The Poetry of John Payne

Volume II - The Romaunt of Sir Floris

John Payne was born on 23rd August 1842 in Bloomsbury, London.

He began his career in the legal profession but thus was soon put to one side as he began his renowned translations of Boccaccio's Decameron, The Arabian Nights, and then the poets Omar Khayyam, François Villon and Diwan Hafez. Of the latter, who he ranked in the same bracket as Dante and Shakepeare, he said; he takes the "whole sweep of human experience and irradiates all things with his sun-gold and his wisdom"

Later Payne became involved with limited edition publishing, and the Villon Society, which was dedicated to the poems of François Villon who was Frances' best known poet of the middle Ages and unfortunately also a thief and a murderer.

John Payne died on 11th February, 1916 at the age of 73 in South Kensington, London.

Index of Contents

THE ROMAUNT OF SIR FLORIS

In this sweet world and fair to see,
There is full many a mystery,
That toil and misery have wrought
To banish from the sight and thought
Of striving men in this our air
Of pain and doubt, and many a fair
Sweet wonder that doth live and move
Within the channel of Christ s love,
And of these, truly, aforetime
Was made full many a tender rhyme
And lay of wonder and delight;
And by full many a noble knight
And minstrel was the story told,
With the sweet simple faith of old,
Of how the questing was fulfill'd

Of that Sangreal that was will'd
By the dear God to Galahad,
And how by many a one. was had
Rare venture in the holy Quests
Albeit very few were blest
With comfort in the sight of it;
And by that menestrel, to wit,
(Oh sweetest of all bards to me
And worthiest to Master be
Of all that sing of Christ His knight
And Questing of the Grail!) that knight
Of Eschenbach, the tale was writ
Of Percival, that now doth sit
Within the bosom of the Lord,
And how he strove with spear and sword
Full many a year for Christ His grace.
And with delight of those old lays,
There long has murmured in my brain
A song that often and again
Has cried to me for utterance;
And now—before the sad years chance
To bear all thought of holiness
From men with mirk of pain and stress
Of toil—it wearies me to tell
Of all that unto Floris fell,
And all his toil and all his bliss
And grace in winning to Christ's kiss.
Wherefore, I pray you, hearkeneth,
The while with scant and feeble breath
I tell to you a quaint old tale,
Wherein is neither sin nor bale,
But some sweet peace and sanctity:
And there not only wonders be,
But therewithal a breath of love
Is woven round it and above,
That lovers in the Summer-prime
May clasp warm hands o'er this my rhyme,
As finding there some golden sense
Of Love's delicious recompense:
For what withouten love is life!
And if therein is any strife,
Or therewithal offences be,
I pray you pardon it to me:
Wherefore, Christ hearten you, I say,
Et Dieu vous doint felicité.

THE FIRST COMING OF THE DOVE

Hard by the confluence of Rhone
A castle of old times alone
Upon a high grey hill did stand
And look'd across the pleasant land;
And of the castle castellain
And lord of all the wide domain
Of golden field and purple wood
And vineyards, where the vine-rows stood
In many a trellis, Floris was;
A good knight and a valorous
And in all courtesies approved,
That unto valiantise behoved.
Full young he was and fair of face
And among ladies had much grace,
And favour of all men likewise:
For on such stout and valiant guise
His years of manhood had he spent
In knightly quest and tournament.
There was no knight in all the land
Whose name in more renown did stand.
And the foe quaked to look upon
The white plume of his morion.
When through the grinding shock of spears
Sir Floris' war-cry pierced their ears
And over all the din was blown
The silver of his clarion.
So was much ease prepared for him
And safety from the need and grim
Hard battle against gibe and sneer
That must full oft be foughten here—
For evil fortune and the lack
Of strength to thrust the envious back—
By many a noble soul and true;
And had he chosen to ensue
The well-worn path that many tread
For worship, all his life were spread
Before him, level with delight
But if in shock of arms and fight
Of squadrons he disdainèd not
To win renown, the silken lot
Of those that pass their days in ease
And dalliance on the flower'd leas
Of life was hateful to his soul;
And so—when once the battle's roll

And thunder was from off the lands
Turn'd back and from the war-worn hands
The weapons fell—he could not bring
His heart to brook the wearying
Of peace and indolent disport
Of ease. Wherefore he left the court—
So secretly that no one knew
Awhile his absence—and withdrew
A season to his own demesne.
And there in solitude was fain
To yearn for some fair chance to hap
And win his living from the lap
Of drowsy idlesse with some quest,
That should from that unlovely rest
Redeem him to the old delight
Of plucking—in the bold despite
Of danger—from the brows of Fate
Some laurel. Nor had he to wait
The cooling of his knightly fire;
There was vouchsafed to his desire.
Ere long, a very parlous quest,
That should unto the utterest
Assay his knightly worth and test
The temper of his soul full well
And sore. And on this wise it fell.
It chanced one night,—most nigh the time
When through the mist-wreaths and the rime
The hours begin to draw toward
The enchanted birthnight of the Lord,—
That in the midnight, on his bed,
He heard in dreams a voice that said
"Arise, Sir Floris, get thee forth.
An thou wouldst prove thee knight of worth!
Gross slumbers of the middle night
So held and clipped the valiant knight.
He might him not to speak address
For slumber and for heaviness.
Again it rang out loud and clear,
So that he might not choose but hear.
And in his heart he quaked for fear;
But still he lay and answered not,
Such hold had sleep upon him got
A third time through the chamber past
The voice, as 'twere a trumpet's blast:
"Arise, Sir Floris, harness thee.
For love of Christ that died on tree!"
He started up from sleep for fear
And groped to find a sword or spear,

Thinking some enemy was near;
But of no creature was he ware.
He saw the moon hang in the air—
As 'twere a cup of lucent pearl—
And in the distance heard the swirl
Of waters through the silence run;
But other sight or sound was none.
The moonbeams lay across the night.
In one great stream of silver-white,
And folded round the Christ that stood
At bedhead, carven in black wood;
And Floris, looking on the way
Of light that through the chamber lay,
Was ware of a strange blossoming—
As of some birth of holy thing—
That in the bar of silver stirr'd;
And as he gazed, a snow-white bird
Grew slowly into perfect shape,
As if some virtue did escape
From that strange silver prisonhouse
Into the city perilous
Of life, and for its safety's sake.
The likeness of a fowl did take.
The light seem'd loth to let it go
Into this world of sin and woe
(So pure and holy) and put out
Long arms of white the dove about.
As if to net it safely in:
But, as the holy bird did win
Its way and through the meshes rent,
The rays of light together blent
And fell into a cross of white,
Whereon the silver dove did light
Above the image benedight
Sir Floris wonder'd at the sight.
And looking on the cross, himseem'd
That from the Christ a glory gleam'd
And lay in gold toward the door;
And something bade him go before.
He rose and girt himself upon
With helmet and with habergeon.
And in his hand his sword full bright
He bore, that Fleurdeluceaunt hight
The dove flew out into the air.
And Floris followed through the bare
Dumb ways and chambers to the gate.
Whose open leaves for them did wait,
And as into the night they past.

Together were behind them cast
The night was dumb, the moon did glower
Upon them, like a pale sick flower
That in the early chill of spring
Mocks at the summer's blossoming,
And over every hill and stowe
The ways were white and sad with snow.
So pass'd he, with the silver dove
That went before him and itbove.
Within the sheeny moon's light—
Wherewith her outspread plumes were dight,
So that it seem'd each wing became
And grew into a silver flame—
Until the hollo'd snow was track'd
Into a woodway, where there lack'd
The moonlight and the mountain-side
With drooping ash and linden vied
To keep the hollow place from sight
Or glimmer of the pearly light.
The dove flew in, and following,
Sir Floris heard a muffled ring
Of silver in the mountain's womb,
As if dead music there had tomb.
Here she with folded wings did beat
Upon the rock that stayed his feet;
Whereat it open'd, and they went,
By dint of some strange wonderment,
Into a place of flowers, all sprent
With jewels of the blossom-time;
And all the air was sweet with rhyme:
There reign'd an endless summer-prime.
Tall green was there of leafed trees,
And in the blossom'd walks the breeze
Was music, such as winds and plays
About the May-sweet woodland ways,
When spring is fresh and hope is clear;
And in the place, where leaves are sere
On earth, there lay great heaps of gold,
Ywrought by wizardry untold
To semblance of the Autumn's waste,
Through which the sweet wind play'd and chased
Its frolic breaths with perfume laden.
In grass stood many a white maiden
That lily in the outworld hight;
And roses all the herbage dight.
Bright plaited beds of jewel-flowers
Were thick-set in the garden bowers,
And many a row of sunflowers stood

Along the marges of the wood,
And to the sapphire heaven turn'd,
As if toward the sun they burn'd
About the blossoms, round and over,
Strange golden-crested birds did hover,
That flash'd and sparkled like a flight
Of winged starlets in the night;
And as they went, their pinions beat
The air of that serene retreat
To rush and sweep of magic song.
And through the trees was sweet and strong
The trill of lark and nightingale.
There was not any note of wail
In song of birds or sweep of wind.
Such as in woodlands calls to mind
The last year's winter and the next,
Wherewith the listener's soul is vext
And thinks how short the spring will be
And how the flower-times change and flee
Toward the dreary month of snows.
The full glad passion of the rose
Was joyous in the garden air.
And every sight and sound was fair
With unalloy'd contentedness.
There could not enter any stress
Of labour or of worldly woe;
But ever through the place did flow
A silver sound of singing winds.
A breath of jasmine and woodbinds,
As if all joy were gathered there
And prison'd in the golden air.
And as Sir Floris wonderèd
At those sweet flow'rets white and red
And at the stream's sweet song, that set
The garden-breezes all afret
With breaking waves of melody,
And at the bird's sweet minstrelsy, —
There came to him a damozel
(How fair she was no man can tell),
And said, "Fair knight, now wit thou well
That thou hast gotten great renown.
In that sad world where trees are brown
And ways are white in winter-time.
And hast in many a maker's rhyme
Been celebrate for gentilesse
And valiant doings in the press
Of armèd knights and battle-play.
In tournament and in mellay;

And over all the land is known
How, many a time, thy horn has blown
To succour maidens in distress.
And oftentimes have had redress
The needy by thy stroke of sword,
So that to him, that is the lord
Of this fair place, the fame has won
Of all that thou hast dared and done
In perfectness of chivalry;
And he, who uses well to see
Great deeds of arms and shock of spears,
Has seen no one in all these years
That may be chosen for thy peer;
And therefore has he brought thee here.
To try thee if thou canst endure
Battle and venture, forte et dure
Beyond the wont of men on earth;
Wherein if thou canst prove thy worthy
He will advance thee to his grace
And set thee surely in high place
Among his knights." "Fair damosel,"
Said Floris, "liketh me full well
The quest, by what you say of it:
But now, I pray yon, let me wit
Who is this lord, whose hest you bear,
That is so high and debonair?
And what adventure must I prove
Before that I can win his love?"
And she, "His name I may not tell;
Hereafter shalt thou know it well;
But thou shalt see him presently."
Then did she join her bended palms,
And falling down upon her knee
Among the knitted herbs and haulms,
Did softly sing a full sweet rh3rme;
And in a little space of time
Was visible among the treen—
Against a trellised work of green
That at the garden's farthest end
Athwart the leaves did twine and wend—
A man, that walk'd among the flowers
As softly as the evening hours
Walk in the summer-haunted treen.
Full tall and stately was his mien.
And down his back the long hair lay.
Red-gold as is the early day.
Whereon a crown of light was set:
Whoever saw might ne'er forget

The sweetness of his majesty.
But in no wise might Floris see
Or win to look upon his face;
For, as he went, he turn'd aside
His visage, as it were to hide
The light of its unearthly grace
From mortal eyes. Then Floris said,
"I pray thee of thy kindlihead.
Fair maid, that I may come to look
On this lord's visage." But she shook
Her head, and "Patience!" did she say.
"Thou must in fear and much affray,
For this fair place and for the fame
Of him that master of the same
And sovereign is, be purged and tried
And many a venture must abide.
Ere thou mayst look upon his face
And win the guerdon of his grace.
And now the time is come to prove
Battle and hardship for his love.
Adieu, sir knight: be bold and true!"
Whereat she sped beyond his view.
And eke that figure vanishèd;
But Floris, lifting up his head.
Was ware of a strange hand that bare
A cross and stood in middle air
And on the white plume of his crest
Did for a moment lie and rest
Therewith great ease was given him.
And healing freedom from all dim
Sad doubt of fortune and of fate
In that great strife, that did await
His proving: and the strength of men
In him was as the strength of ten
Redoubled. Then he saw, beside
His feet, a flower-bed fair and wide
Of roses mingled red and white,
Full sweet of smell and fair of sight.
That in a trellised red-gold grate
Did hold a high and holy state
And spread around such wealth of balm,
Their scent seem'd one great golden psalm
Of perfume to the praise of God.
Then Floris knelt upon the sod
Of that fair place and unto prayer
Betaking him, was quickly ware
How up the silver-spangled grail—
That through the green did twine and trail

Of that bright garden's goodliness—
Some gruesome thing tow'rd him did press,
As 'twere the roses to despoil.
So sprang he lightly from the soil
And from its scabbard iron-blue
His falchion Fleurdeluceaunt drew
And kiss'd its fair hilt cruciform;
Wherewith his heart wax'd bold and warm
With courage past the wont of men.
Now was a loathly thing, I ween,
Made visible to him—that might
Well take the boldest with affright
For up the sward to him did run
A beast yet never saw the sun;
As 'twere a dog with double head.
Whose hinder parts were fashioned
Into the likeness of a worm.
Full black and grisly was his form
And blazing red his eyes and tongue
With raging choler, such as stung
His lusting heart to rob and tear
The flowers that in the garden were.
But as he came anigh the place
Wherein those roses all did grace
The greensward, to his troubled sight
Was visible that valiant knight,
That in whole armour of blue steel
Before the flowery shrine did kneel.
To save the emblems of Love's joy
From his most foul and rude annoy.
Wherefore at him with open mouth
The monster ran, as 'twere its drouth
And ravening lust to wreak and slake
Upon him. Then did Floris take
His sword, and with so stout a blow
Upon the beast's twin neck did throw
The edge, that with the dolorous stroke
The thread of its foul life he broke
In twain, and from the sunder'd veins
The black blood strewed with loathly stains
The tender grass and herbs therein;
And as among the flowers-stalks thin
The hideous purple gore was sprent.
From forth the stain (O wonderment
And grace of Mary merciful!)
There open'd out the petals full
And lovesome of that snowy bloom
That is in all earth's sin and gloom

The fairest of all flowers to see,
The lily of white chastity.
Right glad was Floris of the sight
And of the scent that from the white
Gold-hearted bells to him was lent;
And as he o'er the blossom bent
To breathe its fragrance, suddenly
There came a sound across the lea,
That was as if a lion roar'd;
And truly o'er the flowered sward
There ran to him a tawny beast,
Red-maned, that never stay'd nor ceased
To roar, until the knight could fed
His hot breath through the grated steel
That barr'd his vizor, and his claws
Sought grimly for some joint or pause
In the hard mail, where he might set
His tusks and through the rent veins let
His life-blood out upon the land«
But Floris, lifting up his brand,
Him with such doughty strokes oppress'd
Upon his red and haughty crest,
That soon he made him loose his hold;
And in a while, no longer bold
And arrogant, he would have fled,
But that Sir Floris on his head
With the sharp edge smote such a blow.
The red blood from the rift did flow,
And with the blood the life did pass:
Wherefore from out the bloodied grass
There was uplift the rose of love,
With scent and blossom fair enough,
I trow, to guerdon many a toil
And many a battle in the coil
Of earthly woes. But there was yet
No time for Floris to forget
His trouble in the red flower's sight:
He must again in deathly fight
Be join'd for the security
Of that fair garden's purity.
For swiftly in the lion's place
A raging leopard came, the grace
Of those sweet roses to despoil;
And as he came, the very soil
Quaked underneath him, such a might
To wreak his cholerick despite
'Gainst him that was the sovereign
Of that fair place, and such disdain

Did rage in him, that he could see
No thing for anger. So was he
Against the roses well nigh come,
Nay, was in act to spoil their bloom,
When through his heart the deadly blade
Slid cold; and turning round, he made
At Floris with a vengeful roar.
And with his claws his thigh he tore
A hand's-breadth in his agony.
Then down upon the grass fell he
And died; and in the tender sward,
Whereon his felon blood was pour'd,
The sign of humbleness was set.
The flower that men call violet
Full faint was Floris with the loss
Of bloody that from the wound across
His thigh did run in many a rill.
And would have fain awhile been still
Without reproof. But no repose
Must he expect (nor one of those
That in God's battle fight on earth)
Nor pleasance of delight and mirth,
But many a dint and many a blow
Unceasing, till God will his woe
Be ended and the goal be won.
And so, as there he sat, anon,
Whilst wearily he look'd along
The fair wide path, he saw the strong
Slow travel of a hideous snake.
That with much toil its way did make
Toward the roses where he stood.
So faint he was with foiling blood
He might not summon any strength
To smite its black and gruesome length
At vantage, crawling, but must wait
Until, with slow and tortuous gait,
It won to him. So weak he was.
He could not choose but let it pass
Toward the trellis; and eftsoon.
By him that lay in some half swoon.
Across the grass it slid and twined,
About the grating that confined
The flowers, its black and hideous length
And breathed on them with all the strength
Of hate its envying soul could know
To gather in a breath, and so
To spoil their fresh and goodly bloom:
Whereat the blossoms with the gloom

Of its black coils, that shut the light
From over them, and with affright
And sickness of its loathsome breath,
Came very nigh to take their death.
For with such potent spells the air
Its venom darkened of despair
And malice, that the lovely red
And white of their bright goodlihead
Was to a sickly pallor turn'd,
As if some loathly fever burn'd
Within their hearts: and in a while
No kiss of breeze or golden smile
Of sun had won them back to life.
So spent were they with the fell strife
Of that curs'd beast,—had not a sweep
Of wings awaken'd from the sleep
Of pain Sir Floris and the scream
Of a great bird, whose plumes did seem
To brush his forehead, roused his sense
From the constraint of indolence.
Then sprang he up in strength renew'd;
And when he saw the serpent lewd
And hideous, that in his embrace
Did strangle all the life and grace
From out the flowers, he made at him
And with a grip so fierce and grim
Oppressed his scaly swollen neck.
That with the dolour and the check
Of blood within his venom'd veins,
The snake must needs relax the chains
In which he held the rosery;
And in the act so mightily
He leapt at Floris, that he wound
His arms and body closely round
With scaly rings, and so uneath
Did grip the knight, that little breath
Seem'd in his body to be left;
But, summoning all strength, he reft
The horrid fetters from his breast
And flung the worm with utterest
His might full length against the ground.
There whiles it lay in seeming swound;
And Floris, thinking it was dead,
Would have lain down his weary head
Upon the grass, to take some ease
Awhile. Then from among the trees
There came that fowl, that had awoke
Him with its passing pinions' stroke,

And with so hard a buffet drove
Him down to earth, he could nor move
Nor speak awhile, but lay as dead:
And that foul bird, with eyes of red
And vulture claws, did strive the while
At every joint and crack of mail
To wound him with its noisome beak.
At last a place it found where weak
The armour was, and with such spite
Into Sir Floris' flesh did bite.
That for the fierceness of the pain
He started up from sleep again
And with so fierce and stout a blow
The vulture strake, the steel did go
Athwart the pinions and the crest.
And riving down the armour'd breast.
Did hew the gruesome snake in twain,
In whom the life began again
To flutter. So the loathly two
With that stroke died; and with the dew
Of their foul blood, the lovely green
Of the fair sward did such a spleen
And hate of its despiteous hue
Conceive, that quickly sprang to view
A twine of snow-white clematis.
The sign of sweet content that is;
And where the bird in death was cold.
There grew the glad bright marigold,
That in its gay and golden dress
Was ever symbol of largesse,
Since all along the meads there run
Its mimic mirrors of the sun,
Withouten any speck or flaw.
But none of this Sir Floris saw,
Nor how the roses lightly wore
The freshness of their bloom once more;
So weary was he and so worn
With strife, and therewithal so torn
With claws and beak of that fierce bird,
He lay aswoon and saw nor heard
Or sight or sound Now must I tell
A wondrous thing that here befell,
Through grace of God and Christ His Son:
For, while he lay aswoon, came one
In white and shining robes array'd,
And touch'd him on the lips and said,
"Arise, Sir Floris, whole of wound,
And fill thy quest!" And so was gone.

And Floris started up from ground
And was all whole in flesh and bone
And full of heart the end to dare
Of that hard venture. Then the air
Was of a sudden darkened o'er
With some foul thing, that semblance wore
Of a half bird and a half worm,
Join'd in one foul and loathly form;
And with the rattle of the scales
Upon its wings—that (as huge flails
Upon the golden garnered wheat
With ceaseless rhythmic pulse do beat)
Did lash and wound the golden air—
The songs of breezes deaden'd were.
And all was dumb for much dismay:
And with its sight the lift grew gray.
And as it wheeled on open wings,
With many blows and buffetings
It strove to daunt that valiant knight
And him enforce for sheer afiright
To yield to it and let it fill
Its hungry maw at its foul will
With those fair flowers. But Floris stood
Undaunted, and with many a good
Stout stroke of point did wound the beast.
Wherewith it bled and much increased
Its ravenous rage. Then, suddenly.
He felt sharp claws about his knee.
And looking down, no little wroth.
He saw a huge and monstrous sloth.
Which with such might did grip his thighs
And dipt his arms on such hard wise;
That he could scarce with bended shield
Resist him and uneath could wield
His trusty sword; and as he strove
That monster from his grip to move.
The dragon with so fell a swoop
Against him from on high did stoop.
That down upon the ground he fell,
And in the falling did repel
The sloth from off him. Then the twain
With such foul rage at him again
Did press and buffet, that the life
Out of his breast with that fierce strife
Was well nigh chased: but, by good hap,
It chanced he fell into the lap
Of those fair blooms of various kind
That did his victory call to mind

Against the cruel beaten foes;
And falling heavily from blows
Of beak and talons, he with such
A grinding weight did press and crush
The blossoms in the harsh and rude
Encounter, they must needs exude
From out their chalices the sweet
And precious essences that meet
To make the perfume of a flower,
And on his face and hands did shower
Their gracious balms. So sweet they were
And of a potency so rare
For salving every earthly pain,
The life began in every vein
With their pure touch to run and glow;
And soon the weary weight and woe
That lay on Floris was dispell'd.
Then, with new strength, from him he fell'd
That hideous sloth; and being free
An instant from his t3rranny
And harsh oppression, to his feet
He sprang once more and to defeat
The wingèd worm himself address'd.
That tore and ravish'd at his crest
With ceaseless fury; but it drew
Beyond his reaching, when it knew
Its comrade worsted, and was fain
To wait till it revived again.
But Floris, with a doubled hand,
Smote at the beast with his good brand
So fell a stroke, the sharp death slid
Through bone and sinew and forbid
Returning life to enter in
That loathly dwelling, foul with sin
And sloth;—and so the thing was dead.
And from the blood its slit veins bled
There came to life the blossoms sweet
And gold-eyed of the Marguerite,
Incoronate with petals white.
But that foul serpent with the sight
Of that good blow so sorely grieved
And fill'd with rage to be bereaved
Of its grim comrade was, it threw
All fear aside and fiercely flew
At Floris, with the armèd sting
Of its writhed tail all quivering
In act to strike, and with so strong
A swoop the dart did thrust and throng

Through dent and ring of riven mail,
The deadly point it did prevail
To bury deep in Floris' breast.
Whereat such rage the knight possess'd
That all the dolour he forgot
(Though very fierce it was, God wot,
And sad) and throwing down his blade,
With such a mighty force he laid
To drag that scorpion fi-om his side.
The serpent's tail in twain he wried
And in such hideous wounds it rent.
That from the body coil'd and bent
With anguish it must needs divide.
Wherewith the deft did open wide.
And such a flood therefrom did flow
Of blood upon the herbs below
That needs it seem'd the flowers must die;
And with the pain so fierce a cry
Of agony the dragon gave.
There is no heart of man so brave
And firm but he must quake at it.
And now the doom of death was writ
In heaven for that unholy beast;
And in a little while it ceased
To cry, and down upon the ground
It fell and died; and all around
The firm earth quaked. And as it died.
The blood—that withered far and wide
The herbs and 'mid the stalks did boil
For rage—was dried into the soil;
Wherefore there sprang from out the stain
The holy purple of vervain,
The plant that purgeth earth's desire.
Now may Sir Floris well aspire
To have that peace he needeth so
And easance after toil and woe:
For there is none to fight with him
Of all those beasts so fell and grim;
Nor any sign of further foe
Within the garden is, I trow,
To let him from his victory;
And all around the place was free
From fear; the breezes were a-tune
Again with birdsongs, and the boon
Of scent within the flowers once more
Was golden, nor the heavens wore
The hue of horror and dismay:
And so he may be blithe and gay

And have sweet pleasance. But alas!
No thought of this for Floris was.
Within his veins the venom 'gan
To curdle and the red blood ran
With frozen slowness, as the sting
Of pain went ever gathering
Fresh fierceness through him. Very nigh
It seem'd to him he was to die.
He felt the chills of the last hour
Creep through him and the deathsweats pour
Adown his brow: such agony
Along his every vein did flee,
He could no longer up endure.
Nor hope for any aid or cure;
But down upon the earth he sank
Aswoon, with faded lips that drank
The dews of death, and with a prayer
Half mutter'd in his last despair.
The sense forsook him. So he lay
Aswoon, poor knight, and (well-a-way!)
Most like to die. But there was thought
In heaven for him that thus had fought
For that fair garden's sake. The love
Of the dear God that dwells above
Was mindful of him, though he knew
It not. And so to him there drew
A tender dream,—as there he lay
Smitten to death with that fierce fray,—
And fill'd his thought; and it did seem
To him, by virtue of the dream.
That over him an angel stood.
And with a sweet compassion view'd
His piteous state, and whiles did strew
Soft balms upon him, strange and new
Unto his sense,—so comforting
And sweet of scent, they seem'd to bring
To him the airs of Paradise;
And with their touch the horrent ice
Of death, that bound his every sense.
Was melted wholly; and the tense
And cruel anguish, that untied
The threads of living, did subside;
And gradually peace came back
Into his spirit, and the rack
Of pain and agony from him
Was lifted. So upon the rim
Of the sad soul a little life
Began to hover, as at strife

With Death, reluctant to forego
His late assured prey; and so
The breath came back by slow degrees
To the spent soul, and in great ease
Awhile he lay, and whiles he dream'd
He was in heaven, and it seem'd
He heard the golden harpings stir
The air to glory and the choir
Of seraphim, that stand around
The throne, with one sweet pulse of sound
Coörder'd, lift descant of praise
To Him that is the Lord of Days
And Ancient Then he seem'd to hear
A voice that murmur'd in his ear—
As 'twere a ring of broken chords
Angelic, mingled with sweet words
(So silver-clear it was)—and bade
Him open eyes: and then one laid
Soft hand upon his lids and drew
The darkness from them. So the blue
Of heaven again was visible
To him, as 'twere some great sweet bell
Of magic flowerage in some prime
Of summer in old fairy-time:
And drinking slowly use of light
And sense of life and its delight
Back into eyes and brain, he turn'd
His gaze from where the heaven burn'd
With full sweet summer, and was ware
Of a fair champion standing there.
Past mortal beauty. All in white
And spotless mail was he bedight,
So clear that there is nothing fair
And goodly but was mirror'd there,
And yet no evil thing nor sad
Was there. Upon his helm he had
A fair gold cross, and on his shield
The semblance of a lamb did wield
A fair gold cross. Upon his crest
The snows of a fair plume did rest
And wave; and eke his pennoncel
Was white as is the new-blown bell
Of that frail flower that loves the wind,
And round his dexter arm was twined
A snow of silk. Full glorious
The splendour of his harness was,
And wonder-lovely to behold:
But as white silver and red gold

Are pale beside the diamond.
So was his visage far beyond
His arms in glory and delight
Of beauty. There was such a might
Of stainless virtue and of all
Perfection pictured, and withal
So wondrous tender in aspect
He was, it seem'd as if the Elect
Of Christ on earth in him did live;
That, with glad eyes, men might arrive.
Beholding him, to know the love
And gentilesse of God and prove
In him the sweetness of that grace
Which shinèd ever in Christ's face
On earth. And so in very deed
It seem'd to Floris that the need
Of earth was over, and his soul
Was won thereto where life is whole—
Withouten any stress or dole—
At last in joyance, and his eyes
Did view, in robes of Paradise,
That tender angel of the Lord,
That into men's sore bosoms pour'd
Sweet balms and comfort, being set
To temper justice and the fret
Of life with love most pitiful.
And whilst he thus did gaze his full
Upon the radiance of that wight.
The soft and undefiled delight.
That in his visage held full sway.
So purged all Floris' awe away
And eke such boldness to him gave
That he was fain of him to crave
His name. Then, "I am Galahad,
Christ's knight," he said. Whereat full glad
Was Floris, and all reverently
Unto the earth he bent his kne
Before the knight, and (an he list)
Would fain the broider'd hem have kiss'd
Of his white robe; but Galahad
Did raise him quickly up and bade
Him henceforth kneel to God alone,
That on the height of Heaven's throne
Is for man's soul the only one
Of worship, save sweet Christ, His Son,
And Mary mother pitiful;
And henceforth were no kings that rule
So blest as Floris now should be,

Since that with such high constancy
And noble faith he had withstood
The shock of that unholy brood
And in fair fight had vanquish'd them.
Wherefore for crown and diadem
Of triumph, on the greensward freed
From those foul beasts that there did bleed
Their life away beneath his blade.
In goodly order were array'd
For him those pleasant blooms and fair.
That not alone so debonair
And blithe of aspect were, but eke
Had virtues—more than one might speak
In wearing of a summer's day—
For purging fleshly lusts away
And cleansing from his heart—who wore
Their beauty fairly—all the sore
Sad doubts and weariness of earth,
That so with an immortal mirth
And constant faith his soul was glad,
And evermore sweet peace he had
In love of God and eke of Christ,
The which against all ills sufficed
Of mortal life. And as he spoke,
From the slight stems those flowers he broke
That 'midst the herbage did entreat
The eye with blossom very sweet
And gracious; and (O wonderment!)
Being in his hand conjoin'd, they blent
Their essences in such rare wise.
It seem'd from each sweet bell did rise
A sweeter perfume, and more bright
Their semblance grew, as 'twere some might
Of amity was moved in them—
Being so join'd into one stem—
To heighten each one's loveliness
With all, its fellows did possess
Of blithe and sweet And therewithal,
When from the grass those flow'rets all
Were gather'd, to Sir Floris came
That noblest knight, and in Christ's name,
With fairest look and friendliest speech.
Him of his kindness did beseech
That he from him those blooms would take
And breathe their fragrance. Scarce awake
From swoon was Floris yet; and so
He took them with dull hands and slow.
And did address himself to scent

Their breath, as one half indolent
With sleep; but when the gracious smell
Was won to him, that from each bell
Did float and hovering was blent
Into some wondrous ravishment.
There overcame him such a sense
Of gladsome ease and recompense
Of all his labours, that the dull
Gross drowsiness, that did annul
The soul within the man, forsook
Him wholly; and withal he took
Such gladness, that in every vein
The life seem'd blithely born again;
And through his frame so fresh a flood
Of ardour pour'd, it seem'd the blood—
That in men's pulses sluggishly
Doth throb and flutter—was made free
From earthly baseness and was turn'd
To heavenly ichor. For there burn'd
Within him such a fire of hope,
He felt his soul no more did grope
Within the dreary dusk of earth,
But on the wings of a new birth
Toward the highest heaven did soar.
Nor was there for him any more
A thought of weariness or woe;
But from the earth he rose and so
Was ready for all venturing
And all the quest of holy thing
God might appoint him. Then that knight,
That was apparell'd all in white,—
Most brightly smiling at the new
Glad ardour that did straight ensue
In Floris with those blossoms' scent
And at the holy joy that brent
Upon the dial of his face,—
Within his arms did him embrace
And kiss'd him very lovingly.
Then in this wise to him spake he,
With grave sweet speech. "Beyond the brine,
Where in the Orient first the sign
Of dawn upon the sky is set,—
In that sweet clime where men forget
The winter and the summer lies
So lovingly upon the skies,
That of a truth the very night
Is lucent and the cruel spite
Of darkness never wholly hides

The flowers, but aye some light abides.
Wherefore men call it morning-land,—
A fair and stately house doth stand,
Wherein, by help of God His grace,
Unto my lot it fell to place
That holy token of die Lord,
Which He to mortals did afford
Awhile on earth to look upon
For consolation; but anon.
Moved to slow anger by their sin
And stubborn wickedness, within
His mystery He did withdraw
The blessed thing: but yet the law
Of that sad doom He temperèd—
Of His great grace and kindlihead—
With mercy. For it was ordain'd
That if one kept himself unstain'd
And pure from every lust and sin,
A virgin, he should surely win
And come to taste of that sweet food
Of the Redeemer's flesh and blood,
And unto me such grace was given
That of all champions who have striven
I have been chosen from the rest
For winning of the Holy Quest;
Since that, as in the Writ we read,
God of the humblest may indeed
Be pleased to make His instrument,
Even unto me that joy was sent.
Surpassing all that of old time
Is told for us in minstrels' rhyme
Of Heaven's mercy: and God wot,
Were passèd o'er Sir Lancelot
And sweet Sir Tristram, that again
The world shall never of those twain
Behold the like, such debonair
And perfect gentle knights they were.
Wherefore to God it seemèd fit
That a fair dwelling over it
Should for its safe keeping be built:
And that no breath of sin or guilt
Might there approach, there was enroll'd
A band of knights, in whom the gold
Of virtue had been smelted out
And purified from sin and doubt
By toil and venture perilous.
And in that high and holy house
In goodly fellowship they dwell,

Until to God it seemeth well—
For long good service done—to call
One of the brethren from the thrall
Of earthly life and with His blest
In Paradise to give him rest.
Wherefore, when one is call'd away.
It is ordain'd that from the grey
Of the sad world another knight—
To fill his place who, benedight,
Has won the guerdon of his strife—
Be chosen out, to cast off life
And with much labour and much pain
Be purified from earthly stain
And tried with woe. If he endure
And from the furnace come out pure
Of sin and lusting, he shall stand
For the dead brother in the band
Angelical and shall be set
With those that, pure of earthly fret.
Do guard the shrine miraculous.
In such a wise enrollèd was
Sir Percivale; and Lohengrin
By like adventuring did win
Among the holy knights to sit;
And many more of whom ye wit.
And lately it the Lord hath pleased
That yet another should be eased
Of his long service and preferr'd
Among the angels to be heard
And scent the breath of heaven's rosen.
And in his stead hast thou been chosen
In much hard strife to be assay'd
And for Christ's service fitting made.
Wherefore this venture has been given
To thee, in which thou now hast striven
So wonder-well, that thou mightst win
To purge thyself of earthly sin.
And having in good sooth prevailed
Against all dangers that assail'd
Thee and this garden's purity,
There is great bliss ordain'd for thee;
For that thy name shall be enrolled
Among those knights in ward that hold
The blessed Grail; and thou with me
Beyond the billows of the sea
Shalt come to where that house is fair
Withouten any pain or care,
And shalt awhile taste heaven's bliss

And on thy mouth shalt have the kiss
Of Christ the Lord, that doth assoil
All weariness of earthly toil
And giveth to all sorrows peace
Undying." So the strain did cease
Of his sweet speaking, and awhile
The very sweetness of his smile
Did hinder Floris from reply:
And eke the thought of bliss so nigh
His lips and all the ravishment
Of promise that he did prevent
In his imagining and lack
Of words for utterance held back
His tongue from speaking anything.
But, Galahad for answering
Stay'd not, but, with a doubled grace
Of sweet assurance in his face,
Began to say, in very deed.
That presently there was great need
They should withouten more delay
Toward the dawning take their way.
For many a mile the voyage was
And for great distance tedious.
Then Floris said to him, "Fair knight.
That in whole armour of pure white
Dost serve God in all chastity,
I prithee, lightly show to me
How we may gain that distant land
That by the rising sun is scann'd,—
Since here no manner boat is had?"
Whereat no word spake Galahad,
But with his hand the sign he made.
That makes all evil things afraid
And compasses all good about
With armour against sin and doubt;
And straightway with the holy sign
A white cross in the air did shine
A second, as for answering;
And then the stream's soft murmuring
Grew louder to the sweep of waves
Along the reed-crests and the glaives
Of rushes, and its silver thread
Into a river's mightihead
Was stretch'd; and on the stream did float
The silver wonder of a boat,
Gold-keel'd and fair with silken sails.
Such boat as, in old Eastern tales,
The genii bring at the command

Of some enchanter's magic wand.
And on the prow of cymophane—
Translucent as the pearly wane
Of that fair star that rules the night,
With an internal glory bright—
The milk-white holy bird did sit
And spread soft pinions over it,
That fluttered for desire of flight.
Therein stepp'd Galahad, Christ's knight;
And after him did Floris come
At beckoning, wholly dazed and dumb
With wonders of that wondrous time.
And as into the stem did climb
The valiant knight, the soft sweet wind
That 'mid the blossom'd trees was twined.
Ceased from its disport in the flowers
And leafage of those magic bowers,
And with such strong yet gentle stress
Within the silken sails did press
Toward the dawning, that the keel
Slid through the waters blue as steel
As swiftly as the morning sun
Shears through the mists when night is done
And day is golden in the sky.
And as it through the lymph did fly
Of that enchanted rivulet,
The golden keel to song did fret
The thronging currents, and the break
Of waves on murmurous waves did make
Rare music in the diamond deeps.
Such music as the West wind sweeps
From out the harps of Fairyland,
When elves are met on some sweet strand
Of Broceliaund or Lyonesse,
For revel and for wantonness.
On all sides round them as they went
The dim grey woods were sad and spent
With weariness of winter-time.
And in the fields the rugged rime
Held all things in the sleep of death.
Stem white and void of living breath;
And with the weary weight of snow
The laden boughs were bent and low.
But in their sails a breath there blew
Of April zephyrs, and there drew
Unto their course a summer cloud
With scents of flowers and birdsongs strow'd;
And echoings of July woods—

When in the green the bluebell broods—
Were thick and sweet about their way,
And ever round the boat's prow lay
The scent of grass-swaths newly mown;
And wildflowers in gold grain and brown
Waved in the sweet dream-haunted air.
So went they,—while the night was bare
Of sound or breath to break the sleep
Of winter,—through the woodlands deep,
And past the well-remember'd plains
And towns and meadows, where the lanes
And streets were hush'd with winter-time,—
And saw no creature on the rime.
Save some stray sheep shut out from fold
Or wolf, that from his forest hold
Was by hard hunger forced to seek
Scant prey upon the moorlands bleak.
So ever without cease they sped
Above that swift sweet river's bed;
And truly, as the golden mom
From out the russet mists was born
And all things 'gan to wake from sleep.
They heard the silver rush and sweep
Of waves upon a pebbled shore;
And gliding past the marish frore.
They came to where the river's tide
Was fleck'd with foam, and near and wide
The main, as far as eye could see.
Slept in a sweet serenity.
Far out to seaward fled their boat.
Across the wild white flowers that float
And blossom on the azure leas;
And swiftly as the culver flees
Among the trees with shadow twined,
They left the frozen fields behind
And saw the spangled foam divide
The firmament on every side.
The golden calm of summer seas
Was there, and eke the July breeze
That waves upon the silver foam,
When in the azure heaven's dome
The sign of summer-prime is set:
And still no winds opposed they met,
Nor break of billows in their way;
But through the dancing ripples' play
The shallop sped toward the dawn.
As by some starry influence drawn,
Over the ridges of the main

Unstirr'd and clear. And still the rain
Of blossoms fell about the stem.
And still sweet odours breathed on them
Of rose and jasmine, and the song
Of birds about the sail was strong.
So over silver seas they went,
And heaven, wide-eyed for wonderment.
Hung o'er them open blue the while.
As though all nature were asmile
To see the goodly way they made:
And ever round the sharp keel play'd
The fretted lacework of the foam.
And through the jewell'd deeps did roam
Great golden fish, and cords red
Waved in the dim sweet goodlihead
Of that clear blue; and through the wave
The shells of many a rich cave
Were visible, wherein the sea
Held in a sweet security
Treasures of pearl and lovely gold,
That eye of man might ne'er behold
Until the main should leave its bed;
And over all the deeps was shed
A glancing play of emerald light,
So that the unembarrassed sight
Pierced through the cool sweet mystery
Of folded billows, and the eye
Was free in shadows jewel-clear.
Nor was there anything of fear
For them in lapse of hyaline
Or silver breakers of the brine;
Nor in the crystals of the air
Was anything but blithe and fair,
Sweet winds and glitter of fair birds.
Whose song was sweeter than sweet words
Between the pauses of a kiss.
When lovers meet in equal bliss.
So many a day they sail'd and long,
Lull'd by the breezes' flower-sweet song
And pipe of jewel-birds that went
Above them, fair to ravishment;
Until, one mom, athwart the lift
Of blue was visible a rift
Of purple mountain; and a spire
Of amethyst rose ever higher
Into the sapphire firmament.
And drawing nigh, they saw where blent
Its silver currents with the blue

Of that bright ocean, blithe to view,
A fair clear river that outpour'd
Its waters 'twixt soft green of sward
And slope of flower-besprinkled banks,
Where rushes stood in arching ranks,
Tipt with a jewel of fair flower
As blue as is the morning hour.
When in the golden prime of May
The sweet dawn blends into the day.
The swift keel slid between the rows
Of ripples,—as a steed that knows
The road of some familiar place,—
And past the bubbled foamy race
Of eddies, through the sapphire cleft
Of that bright pass, and quickly left
The billows of the sea behind,
As on that goodly stream the wind
Did urge it far into the land.
Surely was never kingdom spann'd
On earth by river such as this.
Where ever some enchanted bliss
Ran in the ripples, and the stream
With liquid gold and pearl did seem
To glitter. There is nought more fair
Beneath the regions of the air
Than this same river; nor in all
Birdnotes is aught more musical
Than the delight of its clear flow
Across the pebbles, soft and low.
And in the banks were wondrous things,
All lovely creatures that bear wings;
And every precious thing of green.
And flower of gold and jewell'd sheen.
Was there in such a perfect shape.
Its essence must full needs escape
The grasp of my poor minstrelsy.
The very grass was fair to see
Beyond the fairest flower of earth;
For with the gold of some new birth
It burnt, and was aflame with bright
Sweet gladness. Very flames of light
The flowers seem'd, zaffiran and blue
And crystal-clear with wonder-dew.
It seem'd their scent so heavenly was,
That into music it must pass
And soar into a perfumed song.
And as the boat was borne along
The golden ripples, in its speed

Dividing many a woven weed.
That with its many-colour'd mesh
Of trailing leaves and flowers did stretch
And wave upon the waters bright, —
Sir Floris, with what prayers he might,
That gracious Galahad besought
That from his lips he might be taught
What was that river and that realm.
That all earth's sweets did hide and whelm
In one etern forgetfulness.
And made all joys that men possess
Seem poor and naught with the delight
Of its exceeding lovely might
And without pausing, Galahad
To him made answer fair and glad.
"Fair knight, this land through which we pass,
About the city of Sarras
Doth lie; and all the golden plain
Beyond thy vision, for demesne—
By grace and favour of high Heaven—
Unto the Holy Town was given.
Where lies in hold the blessed Grail.—
Before from Paradise did foil
Adam and Eva for their sin,
These happy fields and glades within
The golden gates of Eden were.
Wherein was nothing but was fair:
And this same river of those four
Was one, that of old times did pour
Blithe waters over all the plain.
When life was young and free from stain,
And angels walk'd upon the earth.
And (for their flow) came never dearth
Of kindly fruits nor any drought
Of summer-time the place about;
Nor for the warmth of their clear flood
Might winter nip the flowery bud
Of the perpetual spring, that rain'd
Fresh blossoms there; nor ever waned
The balms of summer in the air,
But evermore the place was fair
With all May-sweets and summer-spells.
And still, — although the cloister'd dells
Of the lost garden no more stand
Upon the peace of the fair land, —
Around its precincts, as of old,
A silver stream with sands of gold
Flows ever, which no foot of man.

Or eye, without Christ's leave, can span;
Of all the four the only one
That still with murmurous waves doth run
In the old channel. Very fair
Its marges are with all things rare;
And over all the land is strown
Thick bdellium and the onyx-stone."
And many another wondrous thing
Unto Sir Floris, listening.
Spake Galahad of that fair land.
That eye of man hath never scann'd,
Save he have won to Christ His grace.
And as he spoke, came on apace
The tender day and gilded all
The ripples; and the golden ball
Of the sweet sun rose high in heaven;
And unto every thing was given
New ravishment and new delight
Of very waking. Fairer sight
Saw mortal never (nor indeed
So fair within our earthly need
Is compassed) than the morning hour
That open'd into full sweet flower
With many a rosy flush and rain
Of golden sunlight over plain
And mead, and many a tender shade
Kiss'd into warmth—that in green glade
Lay waiting for the frolic light—
And changed to fleecy gold the white
Of dawn-clouds over hill and wold.
It was so gracious to behold
The day in that sweet Paradise,
There is no man with mortal eyes
Could drink its beauty wholly in,
For dust of care and mirk of sin
That hide much loveliness from men.
And Floris ever and again
Was dumb with awe of much delight
And wonderment; as with swift flight
The boat sped through the flowers that shone
With blazon'd gold and blue upon
That magic river of a dream,
He sat and stored the influence
Of the lush balms within his sense.
And watch'd the ripples all agleam
With jewels, and the constant smile
Of the sweet sunlight. And the while
The songs of birds co-ordinate

And zephyrs with a peace so great
And sweet upon his soul did seize.
And whiles his spirit had such ease
In that sweet speech of Galahad,
He needs forgot that aught of sad
Or dreary in this life is set.
Or weariness of earthly fret;
And did, without a backward glance.
Yield up himself into the trance
Of that new joy. So sped they on
Toward the orient: and anon, —
Whenas the noon was borne along
The midmost heaven, to the song
Triumphal of the joyous choir
Of birds and breezes, ever higher
Soaring in one sweet antiphon,—
There rose in the sweet sky—upon
The fair broad hem of woven gold.
That marged with many a fleecy fold
The sapphire-chaliced firmament—
A glitter of tall spires, that brent
With an unearthly radiance;
And many a jewel-colour'd lance
Of belfry pierced the golden air
On the horizon; and there bare
The wind to them a strain of song
Ineffable, the stream along—
Faint for great distance—that for joy
And triumph over earth's annoy
With such a rapturous sweetness smote
On Floris, he could neither note
The kingdom's varied loveliness
Nor the sweet antiphonal stress
Of winds and birds and rivulet.
But it alone could hear, nor let
Himself from striving up to it;
For with its melody was knit
About his soul an influence
So strong, it seem'd his every sense
Must press toward it. Nay, at last.
For ecstasy he would have cast
Himself headlong into the stream,
That therewithal, as he did deem,
He might the swiftlier win toward
That wondrous singing and the ward
Of that bright town miraculous.
But Galahad the good knight was
Mindful of him, and by his arm

Withholding him therefrom, did charm
His soul with such sweet words, that he
Must for a while contented be
To wait the progress of the boat.
That very speedily did float,
God wot, across the ripples' race,
To where the turrets of the place
Were clear. And so they came at last
To where the running river pass'd
From the long lapse of pleasant wood
And meadow with enchantments strew'd
Of flowers and sun-gold, and were ware
Of the bright town that all the air
With towers and pinnacles did fill.
Set on the slope of a soft hill.
That in the sun wore one clear hue
Of purple blending into blue.
Most like a great sweet amethyst
And now the gunwale softly kiss'd
The golden shore; and thick with gem
And coral, round the entering stem
Was wrinkled up the glittering sand.
Then Galahad upon the strand
Stepp'd lightly out; and as his feet
Upon the grained gold did meet
Of the rich shingle, there was borne
To them the noise of a blown horn.
That was as if a warder blew
To challenge from some tower of view
Within the amber-gated town;
Wherefrom to them it floated down
And fill'd the air with echoings
So sweet, there is no bird that sings
Could find such music in his throat
Melodious. And as the note
Of welcome swell'd and waned around
The hollows of the hills, — unwound
From his mail'd breast Sir Galahad
A silver horn he thereon had
In its white baldrick, and therein
Breathing, its hollow bell did win
Unto so sweet an answering blast,
It seem'd to Floris that at last
He heard the trumps angelical
Then at the silver clarion's call
The beryl gates were open'd wide
Of the fair town; and on the side
Of the soft hill there was to them

Made visible—upon the hem
Of woven grass with lilies strew'd
And asphodels—a multitude
Of holy knights, that down the sward
In a bright painted pageant pour'd,
With many a waving pennoncel
Of gold and azure; and the swell
Of clarions, co-ordinate
To mystic harmonies, did wait.
With cadences most grave and sweet,
Upon the rhythm of their feet.
So goodly were they of aspect
And in such pictured raiment deck'd
Of say and samite, there is none.
Minstrel or bard, beneath the sun.
That could have sung of their array
As it befits to sing it,—nay,
Not even he who many a day
In Faerie enchanted lay
And learnt full many a year and long
The cadences of elfin song.
True Thomas; nor that couthliest wight
In gramarye, that Merlin hight.
Full bright their arms and lucent were
And of a sheen so wonder-fair,
The sun seem'd of a nobler kind
To glitter, when his splendours shined
Upon the silver-mirror'd mail.
And at the sight of them did fail
Sir Floris' courage, that till now
Had never seen thing high enow
To give him pause; for there did come
So strange a fear on him, that dumb
And cold he grew, and haply might
Have swoon'd indeed for sheer affright
Of wonder and great reverence
That lay upon his every sense.
Forsooth, awhile the blood did leave
Its courses and great awe did weave
Strange terrors in him; and with pain
And fear despiteous, he was fain
To hide his visage from the might
Of that much brightness. Then that knight,
Sir Galahad, laid hands on him,
And quickly freed him from the grim
Sad grasp of that unreal fear,
And bade him that of right good cheer
He should become, for knighthood's sake.

And for his honour comfort take
And new stout heart; for shame it was
And pity, one so valorous
And bold in arms should faint and fail,
Where he most surely should prevail,
'Midst those that now his comrades were
And fellow-knights; and with much fair
Discourse did win him from affright,
So that at last he dared the sight
Of those fair knights and saw they gazed
Right courteously on him and praised
His hard-won victory. So he took
New heart, and with assurèd look
Leapt out upon the jewell'd sand:
And as the twain were come to land,
From those knights all so sweet a sound
Of songful greeting did resound,
The blue of heaven could never tire
Of answer; and from many a lyre
And cithern the alternate joy
Of harpings join'd in sweet alloy
Its silver with that golden song.
So Floris was among that throng
Of knights received, with many a kiss
And glad embracement: nor, 3n¥is,
Fail'd Galahad that he should name
Each knight that to the greeting came.
To him was Titurel made known.
And Percivale, to whom was shown—
With Bors — such grace of God most high.
By reason of much purity,
That they alone with Galahad
Upon the earthly questing had
The blessed vision of the Grail:
Nor Lohengrin to him did fail;
And many another noble knight
Of fabled prowess and approved
In gentilesse and all Christ loved.
Did there rejoice him with his sight.
So, for the meed of his good fight.
Into the wonder-town they bare
Sir Floris,—wherein many a rare
Delight to him appointed was.
Bright was the place and glorious
With glory of the abiding love
Of God and Christ, that is above
All splendours marvellous and fair;
And luminous its ramparts were

With pearls and rubies constellate
And diamonds into such state
And harmony as, save in heaven.
Unto no place or thing is given.
To wear or look on: such a blaze
Of joy was there, without amaze;
For all was easanceful and sweet
With Christ His grace. The very feet
That fell upon the jewell'd stones
Compelled them to such silver tones
Of music, and the ruffled air
Was stirr'd to harmonies so fair,
And for mere passage through the place.
Was won to such a subtle grace
Of perfume, that therein to be
And move was one long ecstasy:
And there the dole of earth and stress
Of hope unfill'd and weariness
Was purged, and life was one delight
Of perfect function, by the might
Unfailing of the doubtless soul;
And every act and thought was whole
In strifeless accord. If one spoke.
The hinder'd voice no longer broke
Into harsh sadness, spent and wried
With weary effort, but did glide
Into an unconstrain'd consent
Of harmony and ravishment
Unstressful; and the every geste
Was with like subtle grace possessed.
And every faculty was cast
In symmetry, what time one pass'd
The portals of the place and heard
The echoes of his feet that stirr'd
The holy quiet. So the spell
Of the charm'd place on Floris fell
Transfiguringjy, as the wide
Gold-trellised leaves on either side
Swung back for him: there came a change
Upon his senses and a strange
Sweet ease of life, as if the soul.
Way-worn and rusted with the dole
And fret of earth, were softly riven
From him, and in its stead were given
To him a new and perfect one,
In a whole body as the sun
Lucent and worthy for the seat
Of the fair spirit Up the street,

Gold-paven and with chrysolite
And jacinth marged, they brought the knight,
Past many a goodly hostelry
And many a dwelling fair to see.
Unto a portal sculptured all
With handiwork angelical.
In stories of the love of Christ,
And all the times it hath sufficed
To win sad living to much ease;—
And passing on with harmonies
Of choral song, they came unto
A vaulted courtyard, stretching through
A cloister'd vista to fair halls
Of alabaster, where the walls
With many a colour'd crystal shone
Of jewell'd casement; and thereon
The questing of the Holy Grail,
In many a wonder-lovely tale.
Was with bright gold and wonderment
Of colour'd jewel-fretwork blent
To harmony, depicturèd.
And there, in truth, Sir Floris read,—
Beside much other venturing
And many another goodly thing
Achieved in service of the Lord,—
The fight that he with his good sword
Had in the wonder-garden fought
Nor, therewithal, was missing aught
Of all that did that night befall
To him: but there upon the wall
Was in bright colours pictured forth
The tale of all his knightly worth
And service. Little strange it is
If much he wonder'd was at this
And could for wonder scarce believe
His eyes, that any should achieve
So vast a work and of such grace
And splendour in so scant a space
Of time. But Lohengrin besought
Him very fairly that of nought
He saw he should be wondered.
Nor any venture have in dread;
Since that to that high Lord, that there
Did reign, all wonders easy were
And wonderless; nor of His grace
Was anything in all that place
That might avail for any fear
Or doubt, but rather to give cheer

And love and confidence was fit.
So sweet a peace did dwell in it
Of amity and holiness.
Then with slow feet they did address
Their further steps,—by a long aisle
Of cloister'd pearl, wherethrough the smile
Of sunlight filtered lingeringly
And lay in one sweet soften'd sea
Of gold upon the silver mail,—
Toward the temple of the Grail.
And in a vestibule, that was
Thereto adjacent, did they pause
And in fair garments clad the knight.
With silver radiant and white.
And then into ap armoury
They led him, very fair to see
With noble weapons, all arow
Against the wainscot. There a snow
Of plumes upon his crest they bound,
And from the swords that hung around
A goodly blade was given him,
That, to the sound of many a hymn
And many a golden litany,
Had in the glorious armoury
Of highest heaven forgèd been:
So trenchant was it and so keen,—
Being in celestial fires assay'd
And in strange dews of heaven made
Attemper'd,—there might none withstand
The thunderstroke of that good brand.
Except his bosom armour'd were
With equal virtue. Then the fair
Graven presentment of a dove
With eyes of gold was set above
His helm,—most like the fowl that brought
Him to the garden where he wrought
Such deeds of arms; and on the field
Cœrulean of his virgin shield
There was a like resemblant set,
That men might know him, when they met
In sharp sword-play or battle-throng.
Then, with a ripple of soft song.
The golden doors were backward roll'd.
That in sweet mystery did fold
The holy place; and Floris came
Into a hall, where with a flame
Of jewell'd light the air was gilt;
And therewithin the walls were built

Of that clear sapphire jewelry
That can in nowise elsewhere be
Save for the pavement of the sky
And for the throne of God most high.
And under foot the floor was bright
With one clear topaz, as the light
Of the sweet sun in hue. Above
There was y-sprad a flower-bell roof
Of that sweet colour of deep blue
One in the spring may chance to view.
When in the golden-threaded moss
The deep wood-dells are odorous
With violets and the clustered bells
Of bee-loved hyacinths, or else
The deep clear colours pers and inde
Of wild-flowers in the gold com twined
With many a tassel of bright blue.
When summer in the skies is new.—
And in the bell were golden lights.
Most like the tender eye-delights
Of the gold kingcups in the green.
That in quaint wise were set between
The fretted azure of the dome.
And therethorough did meteors roam,
As 'twere in truth the very heaven,
And the sweet symbols of the seven
Great angels that do rule the skies
Were therein jewell'd. In such wise
The varied lights were mixt and blent
With those that heavenward were sent
From walls and pavement,—all the air
Was with that lightsomeness most fair
And tender fill'd, that in the May
Is weft about the sweet young day.
When whiles it seems the sky is dight
With one great primrose of soft light,
Most pure and tender. On the ground
There stood fair statues all around.
Deep-set in woven flowers and green
Of lavish leafege, stretch'd between
Tall carven pillars of that bright
Jewel that chrysoberyl hight.
And many another precious stone.
Nor there were images alone
Of holy things, as one might deem;
But eke full many a lovely dream
Of tender love and constancy
Was in dear gold and ivory

With loving hand made manifest
For there was nothing there confessed
Of sin or wantonness in love,—
As ancient doctors teach, that prove
All pleasant things that are to be
Unloved of God. And verily
Sir Floris wonder'd there to see
The histories that makers tell
Of Parisate and Floridelle,
The tale of Tristan and Ysolde,
Of Lancelot and Guenevere,
And many another tale of old.
That men on earth do dully lere
That we should count accurst and ill:
But there depictured were they still.
In very piteous fashion told;
And on the wall in words of gold
Was writ this legend, "Quiconque aime
Complait a Dieu en pechii mesme."
And while Sir Floris stood and gazed
Upon the statues,—much amazed
At all that he did hear and see
Within the temple,—suddenly
There was a fluted singing heard.
As of some wonder-lovely bird.
And then one took him by the hand
And led him where a gold screen spann'd
The topaz paved work of the floor.
Then was he ware of a high door.
That with much wonderwork of gold
And unknown metals was enscroll'd
In many a trellis of fair flowers
And fronds enough fair for the bowers
Of Paradise; and in the leaves
There sat a bird, that was as sheaves
Of ripen'd corn in hue, and sang—
That therewithal the temple rang—
Of unknown glories of the May,
Therein where life is one long day
Of spring and never change is there,
Nor any sadness in the air.
And as he sang, the golden gate
Swung open slowly, and the great
Sweet hollow of a pure white pearl
Lay clear behind that golden merle,
Into a chamber (ashionèd.
There was an altar built and spread
With tapestry of silver white.

Woven with lilies; and thereon
Was set a chalice, out of one
Great emerald moulded,—with samite,
The colour of the heart's best blood,
Enshrouded; and thereover stood
A great white cross and fill'd the air
With living radiance, as it were
A sculptured work of very light
Then with the wonder of the sight
Was Floris fill'd; and for great awe
And reverence of all he saw
Within the pearl, straightway he fell
Upon his knees. But Titurel
With counsel very fair and wise
Required of him that he should rise
From off the ground and without fear
Unto the altar should draw near
And for an offering thereon
Should lay those blossoms he had won
In parlous fight and much duresse,
That of their blended goodliness
And eke their perfume's ravishment,
There might a sacrifice be sent,
To God and Christ acceptable.
And now a wondrous thing befell,
(God grant us all the like to see);
For as Sir Floris reverently
Upon the silver cloth did lay
The holy flowers (that, sooth to say,
Were bright of bloom and sweet of scent,
Unfaded, as when first they sprent
The greensward) and withdrawing thence
A little space, in reverence
The issue did await,—there came
A hand all shapen out of flame,
And from the emerald of the cup
The crimson samite lifted up;
And as this thing was done, there fell—
As 'twere from out the midmost bell—
A light that through the emerald sped
And mingled with the holy bread;
And with the light, came one that pass'd
Thought-swift athwart the air and cast
Himself into the cup,—as 'twere
The angel of a child,—most fair
And awful. Wherewithal thereout
There went a fire the place about,
And fill'd the temple with its breath,

Wherein was neither hurt nor death;
But of its contact there were given
To Floris very balms of heaven
For consecration; and to eat
There was vouchsafed him food so sweet
And goodly such as no man knows.
Then from the chaliced gem there rose
The semblance of a face, that was
With such a splendour glorious
And awful—and withal as mild
And tender as a little child—
There is no bard can sing of it
As it befitteth, save he sit
 (And hardly then) among the choirs,
That to the throb of golden lyres
Do praise God ever night and day
With music such as no man may.—
There is but one of woman born
By whom such aspect can be worn
Of perfect love and perfect awe
Commingled. And when Floris saw
The glory of the eyes and knew
The holy love, that like a dew
From out their radiant deeps was shed
Upon his soul,—for very dread
Of ravishment he could not gaze
Upon their light, but with amaze
And wonderment of joy was fain
Down to the earth to bend again
His eyes: but ere he ceased to see
The vision, of a surety
It was made known] to him (although
He wist not how he came to know)
That heavenly face none other was
Than that same Lord's who erst did pass
Before his vision in the green
Of the fair garden, all beseen
With glittering hair. Then as he knelt.
Unseeing, suddenly he felt
Upon his mouth a burning kiss.
That with such sharp unearthly bliss
His soul did kindle into flame
Of ravishment, the wayworn frame
Could not for frailty sustain
The rapturous ecstatic pain
Of that strange joyance, nor the spright
Embodied 'gainst the fierce delight
Endure of that unearthly boon;

And so for bliss he fell aswoon.
And heard therein a great sweet voice.
That bade him fear not, but rejoice,
For Christ the Lord his lips had kiss'd;
And therewithal the Eucharist
Was borne into his mouth, with sound
Of harps angelic all around
Soft-smitten; nor therefore did break
His charmèd sleep. Then did one speak
To him as in the trance he lay,
And with a murmurous voice did say,
That for the service of that Lord,
To whom was sacred now his sword.
It was ordain'd that for a space
He should return unto his place
Upon the earth, and in all things
That life on earth to mortals brings.
Should for his Master's honour strive,
Until the order'd time arrive
When God should set him free from soil
And weariness of earthly toil.
And there was given him a sign
When it should please the Lord Divine
To make His will beneficent
Patent to him,—there should be sent.
Twice more before the period set
For his release from earthly fret,
To him the self-same silver dove.
The holy symbol of the love
Of Christ and of His chivalry.
And it was told him that when he
Of the white messenger had wit.
He should leave all and follow it:
For when it should of him be seen
Anew, as it of late had been,
He should be ware that God had need
Of him elsewhere, in very deed,
Upon the earth, and will'd essay
His service yet within the way
Of living: but what time he heard
The thrice-said summons and the bird
Miraculous unto him came
A third time, in the holy name, —
He should, in following, be freed
From toil and labour and the need
And weariness of day and night.
And from the knowledge and the sight
Of men be ravish'd, to abide

In that fair town beatified
And serve the Grail, till it seem'd fit
Unto the Lord that he should sit
Among the blest in Paradise
And praise Him ever. In this wise
It seem'd to Floris that one spoke
To him with soft sweet speech, that broke
His slumber not, as he did lie
In that long swoon; and suddenly,
The murmur of the speech forsook
His hearing wholly; nor with look
Or ears awhile was anything
Apparent to him, that could bring
The wonders of the holy town
Back to his senses; but the brown
And fleecy-plumaged wings of sleep
Inclosed him wholly. In a deep
And senseless dream awhile he lay,
Until it seem'd to him the gray
Of night that compass'd him about
Was by a radiance from without
Enlumined and the fluted song
Of the gold merle again was strong
Upon his hearing. Then the dim
Gray webs of slumber were from him
Unfolded slowly, and there burst
A golden light on him. At first
The drowsy cumber on his eyes
Allow'd him not to recognize
The place wherein he was, nor know
Wherefrom the amber-colour'd glow
Of light was borne : but speedily
He was aware that he did lie
Upon his bed, and through the fold
Of silken tapestries the gold
Of the young sun upon his face
Was shed; and past the window-space.
Without the casement, could he see,—
Snow-pure against brown stem and tree,—
The charmèd flowerage of that thorn
That ever on the Christmas mom
Is—for a memory and delight
Of the Lord's birth—with blossoms white
Transfigurate. And on a spray
There sat a mavis brown and grey,
That sang as if his heart were shed
Into his minstrelsy and fled
On wings of music heavenward,

A sacrifice of song outpour'd
To God most high. Awhile it seem'd
To Floris he had surely dream'd
The coming of the dove to him
And all his strife against the grim
Fierce beasts, and all the after-bliss
And wonderment, and Christ His kiss.
But looking closelier, he was ware
At bed-head of his helm that bare
A silver dove with eyes of gold,
That on the crest did sit and fold
White wings above it; and he knew
The holy semblant on the blue
Of his fair shield, and eke the blade
Celestial, by his harness laid
Naked at bedfoot. So the doubt
Was from his spirit blotted out;
And he was surely certified
That verily he did abide
That wondrous venture and had known
Awhile the glories that alone,
For those that many a toil have dared
In Christ His service, are prepared
Within the city of the Grail,
Wherein is neither pain nor wail,
But ever holiness and peace
And ravishment without surcease,
In very perfectness of rest
So hath Sir Floris found his quest;
And so the tale is told and done
Of how, before life's rest was won.
The first time unto Floris came
The holy dove, in Lord Christ's name.

POSTLUDE

Thus far the ancient chronicle
I trace; yet much remains to tell
Of how Sir Floris in the throng
Of men dwelt many a year and long
And wrought great deeds and fair with sword
And spear in service of the Lord;
How love laid hands upon the man,
And how, before the years began
To sap the life in heart and limb,
The dove a third time came to him,

And he was strangely borne away
Out of this world of night and day,
Nor ever more (folk say) since then
Was visible to eyes of men.

And verily the tale stirs still
Within my thought and fain would fill
Its purposed course without delay:
But now, alack! full many a lay
Holds vantage of it in my breast
And hinders me from its behest:
For we who sing, we may not choose
Which we shall take and which refuse
Of all the thoughts to us that cry
For utfrance and delivery:
But, as desire of battle grows
(And will not be denied) in those
That love the long clear-sworded fight
And the sheer shock of knight on knight
Spear-shattering J so the sweet thoughts lie
And gather into harmony
Within their secret hearts that sing,
Until at last the hidden thing
Swells up into a sea of song.
And out perforce the sweet words throng,
Like bird-songs bursting from the brake,
When Spring unkisses the flowers' eyes.
Yet haply, ere the echo dies
Of this my making, I may take
The silver-sinew'd lute again
And in like measures end the strain
Of all that to the knight befell.
Till then, fare joyously and well.

PRELUDE TO CANTO II OF SIR FLORIS

What is there in this life of ours,
Wherein are few of fairest flowers,
But hold within their hearts some stingy
So wholly fair as love-liking?
And what so fit to be the theme
Of poets' lays, in their first dream
And flush of golden minstrelsy,
When not a thing the eye can see
Or thought can deem hut is transformed
By magic phantasy and warmed

To lyric sweetness by the glow
Of youth and songfulness? I trow
It hath been oft reproached to us.
Who in the weary world do thus
With heart and hand seek to express,
In human melodies, the stress
Of song and beauty that amid
The wild waste whirl of life lies hid,
That we too wholly sing of love
And set its sweets too much above
All other sources of delight
And on its radiance jewel-bright
Too fondly dwell; wherefore there pass,
Unmirrored in our verses' glass,
Too many fitter themes of song
And therewithal is done much wrong
And much neglect to many a thing
Of higher worship. We who sing.
We hold there is none other theme
Than this of love; for we do deem
That it all others doth include
And holdeth all in servitude;
Since there is nought that everywhit
Is void of some poor love in it,
E'en in the loathly brood of ills.
That with such sore embroilments fills
Our sordid lives, there is some fair.
In envy, hatred and despair.
Some far faint trace of loves laid waste
And from their proper sphere displaced.
To work ill fortune, as all things
Most high and holy, that one brings
To other than their right fair use.
Grow rank and rotten with abuse
And from a blessing grow a curse,
The better thing to be the worse,
Misused. And if a man enquire
Of aught wherefrom, within the tire
Of this round earthy there may be got
Some glow of pleasance, is it not
Of I/we begot and born of him?
The soft star-shimmer on the rim
Of heaven and all the bright array
Of sun and moon, of night and day,
That holds the halls of heaven above,
Says not our Dante, "It is Love,
"Almighty Love, that moves the sun
"And stars?" The clear sweet songs that run

Athwart the trellis, when the spring
Brings backs delight to every things
Is it not Love makes linnets sing'
Makes brooklets trill and violets blow
And every natural thing below
The sky that is to be most fair
And pleasant? And this Love, whene'er
It seizes on one's heart and hand,
Will not unbind its silken band
Until the thing it wills is done
And its commandments every one
Wrought out with tongue and soul and song.
Wherefore, methinks, the way is long
I have to travel in my rhyme,
Or e'er I come into a clime
Where Love will let me go from him.
Nay, where, indeed, but in the dim
Domain of Death should one abide,
To 'scape his power, the sunny-eyed,
Meknoweth not. And now, indeed,
As I may hope for Love its meed,
There is on me commandment laid
Of that high Lord the heavens that made
And love-liking thereto, that I
Should sing of love and amity.
Wherefore there is no living soul
That I will stoop to his control,
To let me from this theme of mine,
How Floris of the wonder-wine
Of love drank deep and how he won
The fairest maid beneath the sun.
Ladies, have heed; this touches you,
This song I tune my strings unto,
For high sweet striving and delight
And true love between dame and knight.

John Payne – A Concise Bibliography

The Masque of Shadows & Other Poems (1870)
Intaglios; Sonnets (1871)
Songs of Life and Death (1872)
Lautrec: A Poem (1878)
The Poems of François Villon (1878)
New Poems (1880)
The Book of the Thousand Nights and One Night (1882–4) A translation in nine volumes
Tales from the Arabic (1884)

The Novels of Matteo Bandello, Bishop of Agen (1890) A translation in six volumes
The Decameron by Giovanni Boccaccio (1886) A translation in three volumes
Alaeddin and the Enchanted Lamp; Zein Ul Asnam and The King of the Jinn: (1889) editor and translator
The Persian Letters of Montesquieu (1897) Translator
The Quatrains of Omar Kheyyam of Nisahpour (1898)
Poems of Master François Villon of Paris (1900)
The Poems of Hafiz (1901) A translation in three volumes
Oriental Tales: The Book of the Thousand Nights and One Night (1901) A translation in fifteen volumes
The Descent of the Dove & Other Poems (1902)
Poetical Works (1902) Two volumes
Stories of Boccaccio (1903)
Vigil and Vision: New Sonnets (1903)
Hamid the Luckless & Other Tales in Verse (1904)
Songs of Consolation: New Poems (1904)
Sir Winfrith & Other Poems (1905)
Selections from the Poetry of John Payne (1906) selected by Tracy and Lucy Robinson
Flowers of France: Romantic Period (1906)
Flowers of France, The Renaissance Period (1907)
The Quatrains of Ibn et Tefrid (1908, second edition 1921)
Flowers of France: The Latter Days (1913)
Flowers of France: The Classic Period (1914)
The Way of the Winepress (1920)
Nature and Her Lover (1922)
The Autobiography of John Payne of Villon Society Fame, Poet and Scholar (1926)